CREATIVE CERAMIC PAINTING

CREATIVE CERAMIC PAINTING

Cheryl Owen

Jefferson-Madison
Regional Library
Charlottesville, Virginia

WITHDRAWN

David & Charles

WITHDRAWN

3 05477455

A DAVID & CHARLES BOOK

First published in the UK in 2000

Copyright © Cheryl Owen

Cheryl Owen has asserted her right to be identified
as author of this work in accordance with the
Copyright, Designs and Patents Act, 1988.

All rights reserved. No part of this publication
may be reproduced, stored in a retrieval system or
transmitted, in any form or by any means, electronic
or mechanical, by photocopying, recording or
otherwise, without prior permission in
writing from the publisher.

A catalogue record for this book is
available from the British Library.

ISBN 0 7153 0954 4

COMMISSIONING EDITOR *Fiona Eaton*
ART EDITOR *Alison Myer*
DESIGNED BY *Jane Lanaway*
PHOTOGRAPHY BY *Amanda Heywood*

Printed in Italy by LEGO SpA
for David & Charles
Brunel House
Newton Abbot
Devon

Contents

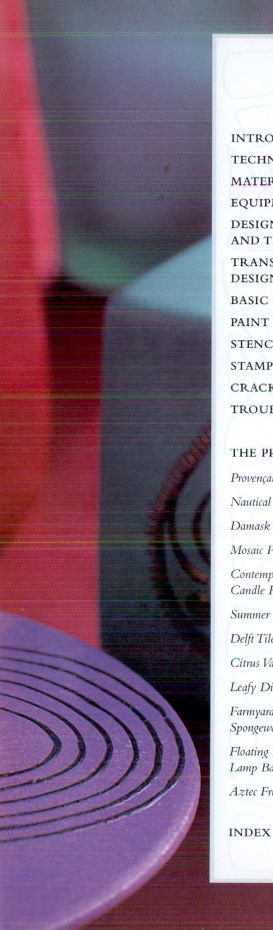

Introduction

Ceramics have been produced in numerous forms across the globe for many hundreds of years, and it is interesting to find that the diverse cultures that created them all felt the need to decorate their clay surfaces in some way. Today, we are blessed with a glorious legacy of ethnic styles and symbols which continue to influence current trends in ceramic design. With the exciting ranges of ceramic paints now available, we can choose to imitate ancient and traditional patterns, making them look as fresh and appealing as they did at the time of their creation, as well as using the vivid hues and easy application of modern paints to decorate contemporary ceramic pieces in completely original ways.

Ceramics are a necessity in all our lives. We eat from plates and bowls, use pots and vases to hold plants and flowers, and light our homes with lamps on ceramic bases or candles in candlesticks. When you decorate ceramics, you can actually use your creations every day. You may be surprised to find how quickly a simple design can be reproduced on an entire dinner service, and the hardwearing qualities of modern ceramic paints will make it a lasting asset in your home. A special project that takes time to complete could become a treasured heirloom.

If you have not yet tried ceramic painting and are keen to start, you will find yourself surrounded by painting opportunities. If the craft is not new to you, there are masses of innovative ideas and new techniques within these pages. Templates accompany each project to help you recreate the designs exactly. Read the introductory section on general techniques as well as the step-by-step instructions, as you will use many of the basic procedures often when reproducing the designs.

Techniques
&
Materials

Materials

Ceramic paints are very economical to use: only a small amount of paint is needed as the ceramic surface is not porous. Start with a small colour range plus black and white and mix the colours to make new shades. Find ceramic pieces at home that can be given a new lease of life by adding a pretty painted motif. Even cracked china can be painted if it is to be used for decorative purposes only: use crackle varnish to give it an antique look.

CERAMICS

Choose non-porous, kiln-hardened china to paint on. If you wish to paint a porous surface, such as a terracotta flower pot, seal it with filler undercoat before painting. Plain white china is often cheaper than elaborately shaped and painted pieces and is the most versatile for painting. Relief designs, such as the fruit-edged cereal bowls on page 49, are ideal for a beginner as the existing motifs simply need colouring. If you wish to paint a design onto a coloured body but cannot find the shade you want, paint the whole piece yourself following the colour-washing or sponging techniques shown on pages 17 and 19.

Before embarking on any ceramic painting project, test the technique and the colours you have chosen on an unwanted piece of china. Ceramic tiles are ideal for this purpose. You may already have some, left over from a home decorating job, but if not, they are cheap to buy from DIY stores. White tiles are best for experiments, and are also useful as palettes for mixing paint and even for making coasters and pot stands.

When recycling ceramics, there is no need to stick to their original purpose. Use a slim bottle as a candlestick or a storage jar as a plant pot. Tea and coffee pots that have lost their lids make charming containers for flowers. Soak stained ceramics in a strong stain remover for 24 hours to release the dirt. Before painting, clean and dry the china well and wipe the surface with alcohol to remove any grease.

STENCIL AND STAMP MATERIALS

Use sticky-backed plastic, which is available from hardware and DIY stores, to make stencils. It is easy to cut and the adhesive backing sticks well to ceramics so that paint cannot seep underneath. Simply peel it off when the paint has dried. Small designs can also be stencilled through shapes cut out of masking tape. If you wish to use a stencil more than once, make it from oiled stencil card or transparent acetate stencil sheet.

Neoprene foam is a thin, lightweight, plastic foam, which is available from craft suppliers, and ideal for making stamps. It is cheap to buy, easy to cut and produces clear, even results. Computer mouse mats, household sponges, pencil erasers, potatoes and even carrots can also be used.

PAPER AND CARD

Keep a roll of kitchen paper handy when painting ceramics; it is invaluable for cleaning brushes and wiping away mistakes. A few sheets of kitchen paper under a rounded ceramic will protect it and stop it rolling about.

Trace templates onto tracing paper or greaseproof paper. If you intend to cut out a template to draw around, cut it from cartridge paper, or from thin card to use it more than once. When making foam stamps, glue the foam to a scrap of corrugated card as a backing.

Carbon paper can be used to transfer designs onto the china. Both carbon paper, used for typing, and transfer paper, which is available from art shops, are ideal. The transferred lines can be painted over or wiped away with a damp paintbrush, kitchen paper or cotton bud.

PAINTS

There are two types of paint formulated for use on ceramics. Water-based paints, often called porcelain paint, can be thermohardened in a domestic oven, which will make them durable and dishwasher-proof. Many water-based paints dry very quickly but some may take up to a week to dry completely. Thin water-based paint with a thinner recommended by the manufacturer or with a little water. Over-thinning with water will lessen the paint's adherence to the china. Solvent-based (cold-set) ceramic paints take approximately two days to set and are for decorative use only – they must not come into contact with food. Clean the brushes for oil-based paints with white spirit or a cleaner recommended by the manufacturer. When painting ceramics, use either water- or solvent-based paints but not a mixture of the two.

Matt medium can be mixed with some makes of paint to give a matt finish, and gloss medium can be added to lighten the colours without thinning the paint. Painted items which cannot be put in the oven can be given a coat of polyurethane varnish for protection, but the varnish will yellow the china. Crackle varnish is applied in two parts to give an antique patina. As it dries, fine cracks appear in the surface. Rub oil paint into these to emphasize them.

OUTLINER

Ceramic or porcelain outliner is a water-based paste that is piped from a tube. It produces a line in relief and is equally effective on its own or with ceramic paints. It is available in metallic colours such as gold, silver and pewter and in a limited range of other colours such as yellow and  red. Do not confuse ceramic outliner with glass painting outliner: the former is more durable as it can be hardened in an oven, making it hardwearing and dishwasher-proof.

ADHESIVES

Masking tape is indispensable. The low-tack tape can be used to stick templates to the china and for masking off sections that are not to be painted. Use all-purpose household glue to stick foam stamps to corrugated card backing and PVA glue to stick jewellery stones to china.

Equipment

You probably already have much of the equipment you will need for ceramic painting. Work on a clean, flat surface. Always replace lids on paints and adhesives to stop them drying out or spilling and take care to keep your materials and equipment away from young children.

DRAWING TOOLS

Use a propelling pencil or sharp HB pencil for drawing designs, and a pencil or fine dark-coloured felt-tipped pen when making templates. The waxy line of a chinagraph pencil adheres well to all ceramic surfaces and is easy to wipe away. A soft lead pencil can be used on some china if it is not too shiny, but test first if you want to transfer a design with a lead pencil to see if it shows up clearly enough. It is sometimes preferable to a chinagraph pencil as the drawing will be faint and can therefore be painted over. Use a ruler or set square to draw straight lines, squares and rectangles and a pair of compasses to describe circles. Use a tape measure to measure curved surfaces.

CUTTING TOOLS

Cut paper, card and fine foam with a pair of scissors or a craft knife. Use a craft knife to cut through synthetic sponge. Always use a craft knife on a cutting mat as the blades will blunt quickly if you cut on a hard surface. Change the blades often, as a blunt blade will not cut smoothly and may tear paper. Use metal cutters or an old pair of scissors to cut fine metals.

PAINTING TOOLS

Although ceramic paints can be applied straight from the containers, you may find it useful to put some of the paint onto a palette to see the colours more clearly, and you will need a palette to mix colours. Use a white ceramic tile, an old plate or a paint tray for this.

Use good quality artist's paintbrushes, ideally with natural bristles. For the projects in this book, you will find it most useful to have a few flat brushes, ranging in width from 5mm/¼in to 3cm/1¼in. These are often called 'one stroke' brushes and were originally used by signwriters. One or two round brushes in different sizes are very practical for both detailed work and for filling in shapes and blending colours. A fine brush is recommended for painting fine lines and details. A 'rigger' is a versatile fine paintbrush: as its name suggests, it was designed for nautical watercolour artists to paint the rigging on ships.

Use a stencil brush for stencilling and stippling large areas and a fan brush for special paint effects. Natural and synthetic sponges are quick and effective ways of applying paint. Always clean brushes and sponges immediately after use. Wash brushes with water if you are using water-based paints, but do not leave them standing in water or you will bend and damage the bristles. Clean brushes with white spirit or a proprietary thinner if using oil-based paints.

ACCESSORIES

Old plastic carrier bags, cut open and laid flat, make a good, water-repellent surface to work on. Although old newspapers are popular as a work surface for painting, they can make the china and your hands rather dirty. Rounded ceramics may need to be supported while they are painted – sitting the piece on a tape reel or resting the edge on a pencil eraser may be adequate. If you are going to paint an entire three-dimensional piece, work on the uppermost area, leave it to dry, then turn it to continue. Use a hairdryer on its lowest setting, held at approximately 15cm/6in from the work, to help dry the paint.

Designs and Templates

Trace-off templates accompany the projects in this book. To use one of these, tape a piece of tracing paper over the image and trace it with a pencil or pen, then roughly cut round the shape. The design is then ready for use or it can be enlarged or reduced on a photocopier to match the size of your china.

DOUBLE CURVATURES

1 Make cuts into a template to be used on a curved surface so it will lie flat against the surface of the china.

2 To check the fit, hold the template against the china so that the cuts overlap or spread open, depending on whether the surface is concave or convex. You may need to make a few more cuts if the curves are very tight. Tape the template in place.

STRAIGHT-SIDED CONTAINERS

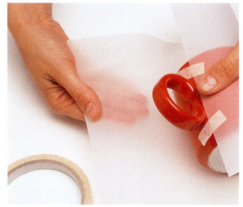

1 To make a pattern, wrap a piece of tracing paper around a straight-sided container, taping it smoothly to the china. Using a pencil, mark the upper and lower edge and the overlap. Mark each side of the handle if you are working on a mug or cup.

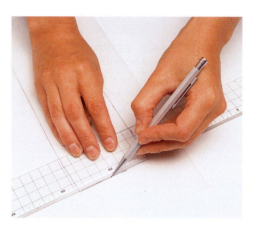

2 Remove the tracing and join up the overlap or handle marks. Cut out and wrap around the container again to check the fit. Adjust your design to fit within this pattern.

PLATE AND SAUCER RIMS

1 To make a pattern, cut a square of tracing paper or greaseproof paper slightly larger than the plate or saucer. Make a straight cut from the edge to the centre of the paper. Place the paper centrally on the plate or saucer and tape one cut edge to the rim. Roughly cut out a circle from the centre of the paper, to help it lie flat. Smooth the paper around the rim and tape in place, overlapping the cut edges.

2 Mark the position of the overlap, then turn the china over and draw around the circumference. Remove the paper. Measure the depth of the plate rim and mark it on the paper by measuring in from the circumference. Join the marks in a curved line. Position the motifs within the paper pattern.

ENLARGING AND REDUCING

1 A photocopier is the quickest way to enlarge or reduce a design. Measure the width of the image you want to end up with. This crab needs to be enlarged to 50mm to have impact on the mug. Measure the width of the original image, which in this case is 28mm. Divide the first measurement by the second. The image should be enlarged to the resulting number as a percentage, in this case, 178%.

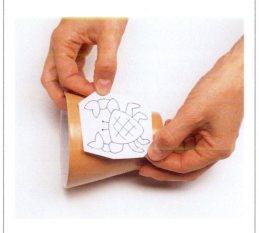

2 Check the fit of the new image against the china. Remember that an enlargement must always be more than 100% and a reduction less than 100%.

POSITIONING MOTIFS

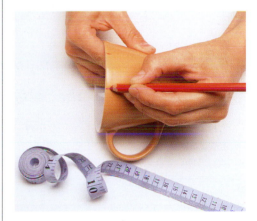

1 To place a set of motifs equally spaced apart, first measure the china, using a tape measure on curved surfaces. Divide the measurement by the number of motifs and mark the divisions on the ceramic surface using a chinagraph pencil. (Wipe away the pencil marks when they are no longer needed.)

2 Tape the motifs to the ceramic surface to check that you like the arrangement. If you have made a pattern for a straight-sided container, plate or saucer, arrange the motifs on your pattern. If a container is to be drunk from, place the design below the lip line.

Transferring Designs

Once you have chosen a design to paint, you will need to transfer the image to the china. Here are a few simple methods you can use.

CARBON PAPER TRANSFER

1 Trace the design onto tracing paper. Place a piece of carbon paper, ink side down, on the ceramic surface. Secure the tracing on top using masking tape.

2 Draw over the design, using a hard pencil, to transfer it to the china.

3 Alternatively, redraw the design on the underside of the tracing using a chinagraph pencil or a soft lead pencil. Tape the tracing right side up on the ceramic surface and redraw it with a hard pencil to transfer the design.

DRAWING AROUND A TEMPLATE

Use this method if you need only an outline and not the internal details of a template. Cut the template from stiff paper – cartridge paper is a suitable weight – or use thin card if you will be using the template often. Tape or hold the template against the ceramic surface and draw around it using a chinagraph pencil. Use a sharp lead pencil when drawing around a template on a painted surface, scratching the outline into the paint.

Basic Painting

Within certain paint ranges, some colours are opaque while others are transparent or semi-transparent. This is because of the variations in the pigments that are used to make different colours. Leave the china to dry completely after painting. Follow the manufacturer's instructions carefully if the painted china needs to be baked.

COLOURWASHING

1 Colourwashing is a good way of painting a large area quickly and is ideal for backgrounds. Use a flat paintbrush to apply the paint, brushing in one direction.

2 Alternatively, hold a flat paintbrush loosely to apply the paint in all directions for a random effect. If you want to intensify the colour, leave the first coat to dry then paint again.

BLENDING COLOURS

To create a subtle change of colour, paint two colours side by side. Then, before the paint dries, drag the colours into one another with the paintbrush to soften the edges. Alternatively, paint an area in one colour and, before the paint dries, add another colour on top and swirl the colours together to blend them.

CERAMIC OUTLINER

Test the outliner on a scrap of paper before you apply it to the china. If the paste has dried inside the nozzle, push in a pin to unblock it. Sit upright and lean forward so that you are viewing your work from above. Gently squeeze the tube as you draw it along the china. If it starts with a blob, wipe away the excess immediately with a

USING MASKING TAPE

To create a neat edge when painting, stick a length of masking tape to the china. Press the tape firmly to the surface and smooth along any creases if applying the tape in a curve. Now paint the china.

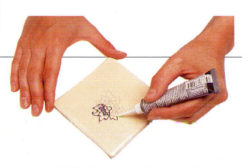

paintbrush. Wash the paintbrush and wipe the nozzle on kitchen paper when you have finished. Replace the lid after use to prevent the outliner drying out.

Paint Effects

There are lots of special painting methods that lend themselves to ceramic painting.
They are all easy to master and great fun to experiment with.

STIPPLING

1 Hold a paintbrush upright to dab the paint lightly onto the ceramic surface. A stencil brush is best for covering large areas. Do not pick up too much paint in one go or you will be left with a dense blob of paint; dab off the excess on kitchen paper.

2 Use artist's brushes to create shading and detail. This is a very versatile way to give definition to your painting. Darken the colour and stipple the edges for shadow or lighten the colour to suggest a highlight. Alternatively, use a different colour for a stippled contrast.

SPONGING

1 Create a mottled effect using a natural sponge. Moisten the sponge with water if using water-based paints or with white spirit if using oil-based paints. Dab off the excess moisture on kitchen paper. Apply some paint to a tile with a flat paintbrush. Dab at the paint with the sponge and dab it at random onto the china.

2 For a more even coverage, use a synthetic sponge to apply the paint in the same way. Always clean the sponge immediately after use.

ETCHING

1 Paint your design and, before the paint dries, draw on the surface with a clean paintbrush to remove some of the paint. Wipe off the excess paint after each brush stroke. The thickness of the line depends upon the thickness of the brush.

2 Use a cotton bud, or even the wooden end of a paintbrush, as an alternative to a brush.

Stencilling

Stencilling gives a highly professional finish on ceramics.
Allow the paints to dry completely before peeling off the stencils.

STENCILLING

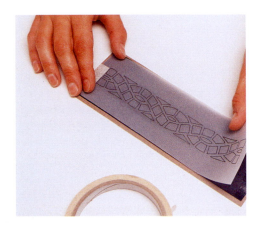

1 Trace the design onto tracing paper. Place a piece of carbon paper, ink side down, on a sheet of stencil card and tape the tracing on top. Redraw to transfer the design.

2 Remove the tracing and carbon paper. Resting on a cutting mat, cut out the design with a craft knife.

4 Using a flat paintbrush, apply a thin film of paint to a ceramic tile or an old plate. Holding a stencil brush upright, dab at the paint to pick up a small amount.

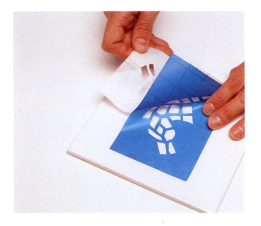

3 Tape the stencil to the china. Or, if the stencil is to be used only once, cut the design from sticky-backed plastic, position it on the china and carefully peel off the backing paper to stick the image down. Smooth away any air bubbles as you work.

5 Hold the brush upright to apply the paint through the stencil, moving the brush in a circular motion. Leave to dry before stencilling another colour on top.

REVERSE STENCIL

1 In this instance, paint is applied to the area around a stencil instead of the space within it. Cut the image from sticky-backed plastic. Peel off the backing paper and stick it to the china. Now paint the ceramic surface, including the stencil.

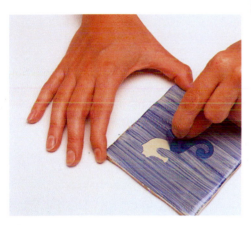

2 Leave to dry, then peel off the stencil to reveal the unpainted shape underneath.

USING MASKING TAPE

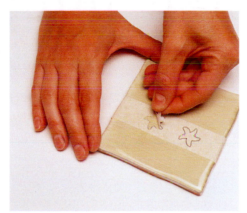

As well as masking off areas to create a straight edge, masking tape can also be used to make small stencils. Stick the tape down firmly. Draw the motifs on top and cut them out with a craft knife. Carefully peel off the motifs and stencil the cut-outs. Leave to dry, then peel off the tape.

Stamping

Stamping works best on simple shapes where tight definition is not needed. Experiment with the variety of materials you can use to make your own stamps, as well as with ready-made stamps.

MAKING YOUR OWN STAMP

1 Cut out the template from paper and draw around it on neoprene foam. Cut out the shape with a craft knife or a pair of scissors. Stick the foam shape to a piece of corrugated card using all-purpose household glue. Leave to dry.

2 Trim the card around the foam, leaving a border of 5mm/¼in. This will enable you to hold the stamp without smudging and will act as a guide when positioning it.

4 Press the stamp firmly onto the ceramic surface then lift it off cleanly. Wipe the foam clean immediately after use and between colours.

3 Paint the stamp evenly using a paintbrush. Do not apply the paint too thickly or it will seep out when stamping and the image will be distorted.

SYNTHETIC SPONGE STAMP

Alternatively, cut a stamp from a synthetic sponge. A kitchen sponge backed with a scourer has a good texture for this and is cheap and easily available. Draw the image on the scourer side of the sponge and cut it out using a craft knife. Do not use scissors as they will distort the design on thick sponge. Use the sponge side for stamping.

POTATO STAMP

1 Cut a small potato in half or a large potato into thick slices. Cut out the template from paper and draw around it on the flat face of the potato using a waterproof marker pen. Hold a knife upright to cut along the outline.

2 Hold the knife horizontally to cut around the potato, approximately 5mm/¼in below the surface. Pull off the cut pieces of potato, leaving the image standing proud. Trim the edges of the potato, leaving a border of about 5mm/¼in surrounding the design. This gives you something to hold and will help you judge the positioning of the stamp.

3 Paint the surface of the stamp and leave to dry to seal the porous surface. Paint the stamp again and press onto the china. Lift it off cleanly and repaint it to continue.

Crackle Varnish

Crackle varnish is suitable only for decorative ceramics and must not come into contact with food. Use it to give an antique patina to objects such as lamps, vases and plant pots.

 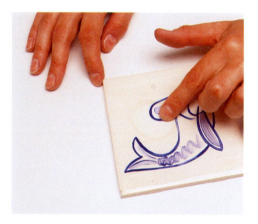 

1 Leave the painted china to dry overnight, then apply a coat of polyurethane varnish to seal the surface. Following the manufacturer's instructions, apply the first part of the crackle varnish, which is oil-based. Like polyurethane varnish, it will yellow the ceramic surface. Leave to dry until it is barely 'tacky'. The length of time needed depends upon the temperature and the thickness of the varnish. If left to dry overnight the varnish will be almost dry and the cracks very small.

2 Apply the second part of the varnish, which is water-based. After a few minutes, rub the surface gently with your fingertips. This will fill in any gaps and remove any brush marks.

3 Allow to dry for a few hours. Gently heat the surface with a hairdryer held about 15cm/6in from the china or place it close to a radiator. This will hasten the drying time of the second coat and you will see fine cracks appear.

4 To emphasize the cracks, rub in burnt umber oil paint using kitchen paper. Wipe off the excess paint with a clean piece of kitchen paper. Leave to dry overnight then apply a further coat of polyurethane varnish to seal the surface.

Trouble-shooting

Although ceramic painting techniques are simple, it is best to practise on an old piece of china first. If you do make a mistake, the paint can be rubbed away with moistened kitchen paper or a cotton bud: it is best to do this sooner rather than later.

REMOVING TRANSFERS

Some transferred lines can be painted over but some will show through the paint and must be removed just before painting. Before you paint a section, rub away pencil lines with kitchen paper or a cotton bud, using clean paper or a new bud for each application. Wipe away lines transferred using carbon paper with a damp paintbrush or moistened cotton bud.

RELEASING STENCILS

Once the paint has dried, peel off stencils and masking tape carefully. If the paint starts to come away as well, press the stencil or tape back down and run a craft knife along the edge to cut through the paint. The stencil and tape will then come away smoothly.

NEATENING EDGES

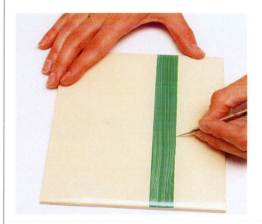

With the tip of a craft knife blade, gently scratch away any paint that has seeped under the edge of a stencil or masking tape to give a neat edge.

LOW-TACK MASKING TAPE

You may need to stick masking tape on areas that have already been painted. Although the tape is low-tack, it is prone to lifting off paint when it is pulled away. Before sticking tape onto a painted area, stick it to your clothing a few times to lessen its adhesive qualities – but stick it to woven fabric rather than woollens or you will transfer fluff to the china.

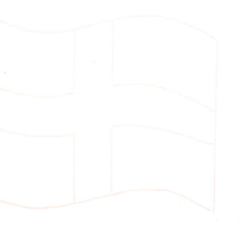

The Projects

Provençal Canister

The clear, warm colours and traditional designs of Provençal style will introduce a ray of sunshine into your kitchen at all times of the year. Stylized floral motifs characterize the look, in colours that, though brilliant, reflect their origins in natural dyes and pigments. Team decorated ceramics with pretty printed fabrics and some authentic enamelled accessories to give a room a flavour of the French countryside. This storage canister in a wonderful buttery yellow embodies the rustic style when it is embellished with a traditional motif repeated along a band of bright blue.

Materials & Equipment

MASKING TAPE

YELLOW CERAMIC CANISTER

TRACING PAPER

HARD AND SOFT PENCILS

SCISSORS

KITCHEN PAPER

CHINAGRAPH PENCIL

RULER

CERAMIC PAINTS: WHITE, RED, GREEN, BLUE, BLACK AND YELLOW

WHITE CERAMIC TILE, OLD PLATE OR MIXING TRAY

MEDIUM AND FINE PAINTBRUSHES

CIRCULAR TEMPLATE, SUCH AS A JAM JAR LID

1 Apply two strips of masking tape around the top of the canister, leaving a 4cm/1½in gap between them. Trace the plaque motif onto tracing paper and cut out to use as a template. Lay the canister on its side on a few sheets of kitchen paper. Using a chinagraph pencil, draw around the template eight times between the masked lines, spacing the plaques evenly.

2 With the canister still on its side, paint the uppermost plaques white. Leave to dry then turn the canister to paint the rest.

6 Using a chinagraph pencil, draw wavy stems between the flowers, from the blue band to the base of the canister. Paint the stems green using a fine paintbrush. Add green leaves to the stems. Edge the blue band with a row of red dots then highlight it with a yellow dot between each plaque.

3 Trace the flower on the plaque template. Rub over the back of the tracing with a soft pencil and draw round the design to transfer it to each painted plaque. Paint the flowers red, again painting those that are uppermost first, then turning the canister to continue.

4 Use a very fine paintbrush to paint the stems green. Apply a ring of green dots to each petal then dot the top half of each plaque at random with black paint.

5 Paint the background between the masked lines blue. Make sure the first area of paint has dried before turning the canister to continue the painting. Peel off the masking tape when the paint has dried.

7 Using a small circular template such as a jam jar lid, draw a circle on the lid with a chinagraph pencil and paint it green to match the stems, adding some leaves as before. Leave to dry.

Nautical Platter

This smart platter with its border of signalling

flags would make a grand gift for a sailor. Each flag

stands for a letter of the alphabet: if you know the

code, you could spell out a name, or even a cheeky

message, around the dish! The decoration is painted

using a reverse stencilling technique: the flag shapes are

masked out while the background is painted in a pale

wash of blue and turquoise which evokes a calm sea.

The primary colours and strong shapes on

the flags provide a vibrant contrast.

Materials & Equipment

MASKING TAPE

WHITE CERAMIC OVAL PLATTER

TRACING PAPER

PENCIL

STICKY-BACKED PLASTIC

SCISSORS

CERAMIC PAINTS: WHITE, BLUE,
TURQUOISE, RED AND YELLOW

WHITE CERAMIC TILE,
OLD PLATE OR MIXING TRAY

WIDE FLAT AND MEDIUM
PAINTBRUSHES

KITCHEN PAPER

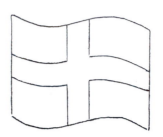 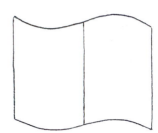

1 Apply a length of masking tape to the platter just inside the rim. Press the tape firmly to the surface of the china.

2 Trace the flag shape and cut out a paper template. Draw around it on the paper backing of the sticky-backed plastic. Cut out 14 flags. Tape them, evenly spaced, around the rim. Peel off the backing paper and stick the flags in place.

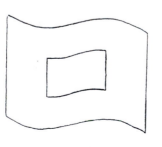 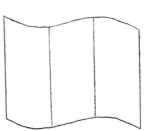 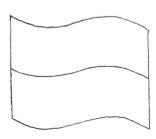

3 Mix white with blue, and white with turquoise paint. Use a wide, flat paintbrush to paint the rim, alternating and overlapping the colours and brushing the paint outwards from the taped edge.

4 Leave to dry, then peel off the tape and flag shapes. Refer to the photograph on page 33 to paint the flags red, yellow and blue, leaving the white areas unpainted. Allow to dry, then bake the platter to harden the paint if necessary, following the paint manufacturer's instructions.

Damask Tea Set

This flowing design of stylized pomegranates and flowers is influenced by the classic motifs found on damask fabrics, which are as popular today as they were when first designed centuries ago. The Florentine weavers of early damasks borrowed these exuberant patterns from Persian carpets. Your own damask tablecloth will make a perfect setting for this pretty gilded tea set. You will need to make templates to fit your own cup and saucer: see how to do this on pages 14–15. Fold the saucer template in half, then enlarge or reduce the images to fit within your outlines. Remember to place the motifs below the lip line on the cup.

Materials & Equipment

TRACING PAPER

PENCIL

CARBON PAPER

STAPLER

SCISSORS

STRAIGHT-SIDED TEA CUPS
AND SAUCERS

MASKING TAPE

SUPPORT, SUCH AS
A TAPE REEL

FINE PAINTBRUSH

CERAMIC PAINT: GOLD

COTTON BUD (OPTIONAL)

KITCHEN PAPER

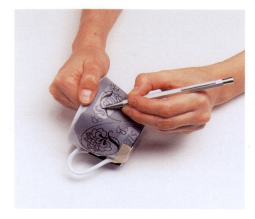

1 Trace the cup design once and the saucer design twice onto tracing paper. Place the tracings on a sheet of carbon paper, with the carbon ink side down. Staple together, then cut out the designs. Wrap the carbon template, ink side down, around the cup. Position the tracing on top and tape to the cup.

2 Redraw the design lightly with a pencil to transfer the image. Remove the tracing and carbon paper. Rest the edge of the cup on a support such as a tape reel ready for painting. (If the cup is laid directly on the work surface, the transferred image on the underside may smudge.)

Cup Template

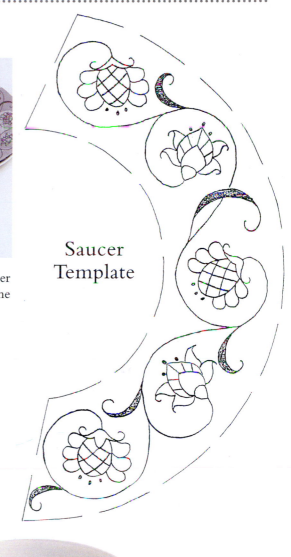

Saucer
Template

3 Use a fine paintbrush to apply gold ceramic paint thickly along the outlines. If the carbon has transferred very densely, wipe away the area you are about to paint with a cotton bud or a moistened paintbrush before painting or it may show through the paint. Leave the first section to dry, then turn the cup to continue painting.

4 Position the carbon paper for the saucer ink side down on the rim, then tape the tracings on top. Redraw lightly with a pencil to transfer the design.

5 Remove the tracings and carbon paper. Paint the saucer to match the cup. Leave to dry, then bake the china to harden the paint if necessary, following the paint manufacturer's instructions.

Mosaic Planter

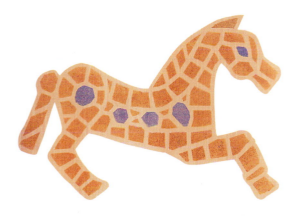

The realistic mosaic effect on this classic planter

is achieved by stencilling. A noble horse, which is

Roman in style, is worked in colours reminiscent of

the elaborate mosaic flooring of Italianate villas.

Choose a planter that is plain in shape: this one has flat,

square sides, which are ideal for this style of decoration

and easy to work on using a large stencil. Originally

white, it was first colourwashed in light brown to give

a soft background colour to the mosaic work. You

could use a pot that is already coloured, as long as

it is not too rich or dark. The same design is

painted on all four sides.

Materials & Equipment

CERAMIC PAINTS: WHITE,
BROWN, DARK BLUE AND BLACK

WHITE CERAMIC TILE,
OLD PLATE OR MIXING TRAY

18CM/7¼IN SQUARE WHITE
CERAMIC PLANTER

WIDE FLAT PAINTBRUSH

SCISSORS

TRACING PAPER

CARBON PAPER

STENCIL CARD OR
ACETATE SHEET

PENCIL

MASKING TAPE

CRAFT KNIFE

CUTTING MAT

STENCIL BRUSH

KITCHEN PAPER

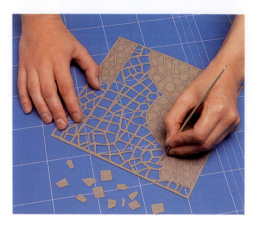

1 Mix brown and white paint together and paint one side of the planter using a wide, flat paintbrush. Set aside to dry then turn the piece to paint the other sides.

2 Cut 18cm/7¼in squares of tracing paper, carbon paper and stencil card or acetate sheet. Enlarge the design to 18cm/7¼in and trace it onto the tracing paper. Place the carbon paper, ink side down, on the stencil card and place the tracing on top. Tape in place and redraw the design to transfer the image. Remove the papers and cut out the shapes on the stencil with a craft knife on a cutting mat.

3 Mask off the areas around the background mosaics, which will be stencilled white, then tape the stencil to the front of the planter. Apply a thin film of white paint to an old plate or a ceramic tile using a flat paintbrush. Holding a stencil brush upright, dab at the paint then move the brush in a circular motion to apply the paint through the stencil. Leave to dry then lightly stencil brown paint on top of the white areas, to give a slightly distressed look. Leave to dry then repeat on the other sides of the planter.

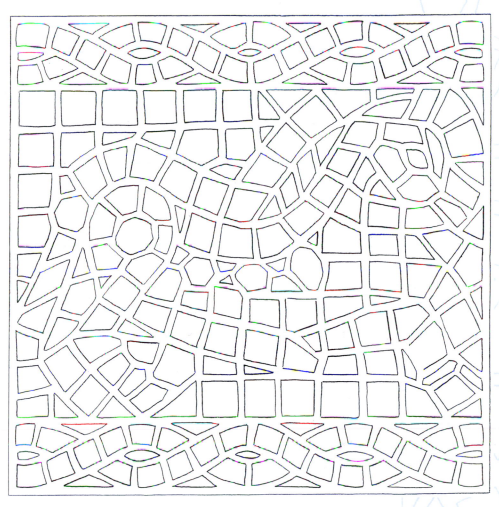

4 Unpeel the masking tape. Mask the areas surrounding the horse, the wavy border, and the details on the horse. Stencil the horse and border background brown, lining the stencil up with the areas already painted. Repeat on the other sides. Unpeel the tape and mask around the wavy border and details on the horse. Mix white, dark blue and black paint together and stencil the border and details. Repeat on the other sides and remove the stencil. Bake the planter if necessary to harden the paint, following the paint manufacturer's instructions.

Contemporary Candle Holders

The neat lines of these candle holders lend themselves to simple designs and are a great project to tackle if you are a beginner and want to try out a few techniques. The overall background colours have been applied with a synthetic sponge to give a quick, even coverage of colour. Jewellery stones, such as the one applied to the square candle holder, are available from craft and haberdashery stores and give a professional touch to the piece. Pewter-coloured ceramic outliner was used to apply the patterns to the painted china, to give a subtle three-dimensional effect.

Materials & Equipment

CERAMIC PAINTS: MAUVE, WHITE, BRIGHT GREEN AND PALE PINK

WHITE CERAMIC TILE, OLD PLATE OR MIXING TRAY

FLAT PAINTBRUSHES

SYNTHETIC SPONGE

ROUND AND SQUARE WHITE CERAMIC CANDLE HOLDERS

SCISSORS

PAIR OF COMPASSES

PAPER

PENCIL

CERAMIC OUTLINER: PEWTER

1CM/1/2IN MASKING TAPE

LILAC CABOUCHON JEWELLERY STONE

PVA GLUE

KITCHEN PAPER

1 Mix mauve and white paint together to make lilac. Paint onto the sponge. Dab the sponge all over the round candle holder. Leave to dry.

2 Cut a 5.5cm/2¼in diameter circle of paper. With a pencil, draw around the circle a few times on the round candle holder, positioning the template so it extends beyond the surface and you are only drawing sections of the circles. Draw along the outlines with pewter outliner, then draw circles of decreasing size freehand within the outlines.

4 Paint the stripe pale pink using a flat paintbrush. Draw the teardrop on paper and cut it out. Draw around the template on one side of the candle holder. Stick the jewellery stone in the middle of the teardrop shape using PVA glue.

3 Stick a length of masking tape around the square candle holder at one edge. Mix bright green and white paint together. Paint onto a synthetic sponge and dab all over the candle holder. Leave to dry then carefully peel off the tape.

5 Allow the glue to dry, then outline the jewellery stone with pewter outliner. Draw along the teardrop outline with the outliner and then draw a simple design freehand within the teardrop and along the pink stripe. Set aside to dry.

Summer Fruit Bowls

This is an ideal project to try if you are new to painting ceramics, because the design is already in place – you just need to add colour. Look out for some pretty white tableware decorated with simple relief motifs: there are lots of ranges available, such as these breakfast bowls with a border of summer fruits. You can buy a few pieces at a time and enlarge your collection as you perfect your technique. Painting the relief designs turns mass-produced china into something that has a handcrafted appeal.

Materials & Equipment

CERAMIC PAINTS: YELLOW,
WHITE, ORANGE, RED,
TWO SHADES OF GREEN, BLACK,
FUCHSIA PINK AND BROWN

WHITE CERAMIC TILE,
OLD PLATE OR MIXING TRAY

MEDIUM AND FINE
PAINTBRUSHES

WHITE CEREAL BOWLS WITH
A RELIEF BORDER

KITCHEN PAPER

1 Mix yellow and white paint to make a pale lemon yellow and paint the lemons. Then paint one edge of each fruit in a brighter yellow to create a shadow and enhance the shape.

2 Mix orange, red and yellow paint together for the oranges, blending the colours on the bowl. Paint one half of each pear green and the other half yellow mixed with a little white, then blend the colours together.

3 Mix black and fuchsia pink paint together to make a deep purple and dot it on to the bunches of grapes.

4 Paint the lemon, orange and pear leaves mid-green, and use a darker shade for the vine leaves.

5 Use dark brown paint to pick out the stalks and dot the base of each orange. Leave to dry. Bake the bowls to harden the paint if necessary, following the paint manufacturer's instructions.

Delft Tiles

Delft tiles, with their charming, naïvely painted motifs, have a timeless quality which makes them suitable for many applications and all kinds of different settings. Their classic, cobalt blue and white colouring always looks fresh and pretty. This set of tiles has been painted with a range of traditional floral designs; you could use them individually as pot stands or paint enough to tile a splashback or tabletop. If you wish to tile a large area, paint some tiles with just the corner motifs.

Materials & Equipment

TRACING PAPER

HARD AND SOFT PENCILS

15CM/6IN WHITE GLAZED TILES

MASKING TAPE

CERAMIC PAINTS: DARK BLUE,
MID BLUE, PALE BLUE AND WHITE

WHITE CERAMIC TILE,
OLD PLATE OR MIXING TRAY

FINE PAINTBRUSHES

KITCHEN PAPER

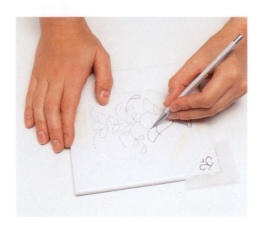

1 Trace one of the flower designs and the corner motif. Trace over the back of the flower with a soft pencil. Position it centrally on a white tile, securing it with masking tape. Carefully draw over the lines again, using a hard pencil, to transfer the design. Remove the tracing. Apply the corner motif in each corner in the same way, matching the broken lines to the tile edges.

2 Use a fine paintbrush to paint the outline of the central design in dark blue paint. Paint the dark leaves and the base of the vase.

5 Paint the corner motifs in dark blue using a fine paintbrush. Leave to dry.

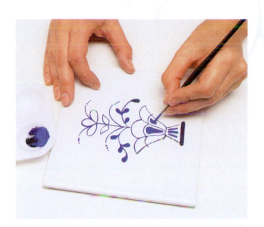

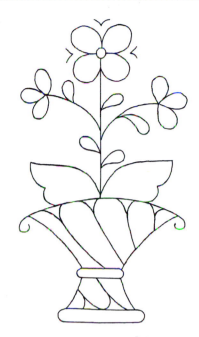

3 Using mid blue, fill in some areas of the design with a slightly larger paintbrush. Do not paint right up to the edges of the dark blue outlines. Add small dots of mid blue for buds.

4 Complete the motif with some touches of light blue.

Citrus Vase

This striking vase is decked with tangy slices of

oranges and lemons, making it the perfect container

for vibrantly coloured summer flowers. A strong

turquoise provides an excellent contrast as the

background colour. Although the effect is very bold,

no special painting skills are needed. The circular motifs

are outlined with citrus shades and the fruit segments

are painted freehand. The missing segments in some

of the fruit slices, and the subtle texture of the

background, achieved with random strokes of a flat

brush, give this simple design extra zing.

Materials & Equipment

PAIR OF COMPASSES

PAPER

SCISSORS

MASKING TAPE

WHITE CERAMIC VASE

CHINAGRAPH PENCIL

FLAT PAINTBRUSHES

CERAMIC PAINTS: ORANGE, YELLOW, WHITE AND TURQUOISE

WHITE CERAMIC TILE, OLD PLATE OR MIXING TRAY

KITCHEN PAPER

1 Describe 7cm/2¾in diameter circles on paper and cut them out to use as templates for the fruit slices. Cut 'V' shapes out of some of the circles. Tape the templates to the vase.

2 Draw around the templates using a chinagraph pencil and then remove them.

5 To help paint evenly sized segments, first lightly paint the edges of a cross in the centre of each slice and use it as a guide to paint eight segments the same colour as the rind. Leave to dry then rub away any visible pencil marks.

3 Use a 5mm/¼in flat paintbrush to paint around the circumference of each circle for the rind of the fruit. Use orange paint for the oranges and yellow for the lemons. Leave to dry.

4 Mix yellow and white paint together for the pith. Use the same paintbrush to paint a line inside the rind.

6 Paint the background turquoise using a flat paintbrush. Set aside to dry, then bake the vase to harden the paint if necessary, following the paint manufacturer's instructions.

Leafy Dinner Plates

You probably last tried leaf printing during your

earliest schooldays, but it can be used very effectively

with ceramic paints to produce these elegant designs

on plain coloured plates. Choose leaves that have

interesting shapes but are not too intricate or large, and

try to find perfect specimens. These plates were selected

because their colours toned naturally with the realistic

paint colours used on the leaves. Remember that you

can colourwash your plates before printing with the

leaves to get exactly the background colour you want.

Materials & Equipment

FRESH LEAVES

YELLOW AND GREEN
CERAMIC PLATES

CHINAGRAPH PENCIL

CERAMIC TILE OR OLD PLATE

CERAMIC PAINTS: SAGE GREEN
AND BRIGHT GREEN

FLAT AND FINE PAINTBRUSHES

KITCHEN PAPER

1 Hold a leaf centrally against the plate and mark its position at the top and bottom with a chinagraph pencil. This will help you place it correctly when printing.

2 Resting on a ceramic tile or an old plate, paint the underside of the leaf evenly.

3 Carefully place the leaf, paint side down, on the plate between your alignment marks. Press down firmly with a sheet of kitchen paper, which will soak up any excess paint. Gently peel off the leaf.

4 Leave to dry, then paint on some delicate veins with a fine paintbrush, using the same colour paint as used on the leaf. Set aside to dry then bake the plates if necessary to harden the paint, following the paint manufacturer's instructions.

Farmyard Spongeware Jug

Spongeware was originally made in Staffordshire in the 18th century. The simplicity and immediacy of the folk art designs proved very popular and spongeware was soon being produced in other areas of Great Britain and the United States, and was exported worldwide. It is once more in vogue today, and potteries continue to decorate ceramics by hand in this traditional fashion, using stencils for the repeated motifs which are sponged in a limited palette of soft colours. Though originally sold cheaply as kitchenware, antique examples now fetch high prices. This proud cockerel jug could become an heirloom for the future.

Materials & Equipment

CERAMIC PAINTS: WHITE, BROWN,
ORANGE, RED, GREY AND BLUE

WHITE CERAMIC TILE
OR OLD PLATE

FLAT, MEDIUM AND FINE
PAINTBRUSHES

NATURAL SPONGE

WATER OR WHITE SPIRIT

WHITE CERAMIC JUG

TRACING PAPER

PENCIL

SCISSORS

SYNTHETIC SPONGE

CRAFT KNIFE

CUTTING MAT

COTTON BUD

KITCHEN PAPER

1 Mix white with a little brown and orange paint. Apply to a ceramic tile or an old plate with a flat paintbrush. Lightly moisten a natural sponge, with water if using water-based paints and white spirit if using oil-based paints. Dab at the paint with the sponge then sponge the jug lightly all over. Leave to dry.

5 Cut a 1.5cm/⅝in square from a synthetic sponge. Paint the sponge blue. Starting at the centre of the spout, stamp a row of squares 1.5cm/⅝in apart, close to the upper edge. Repeat close to the base.

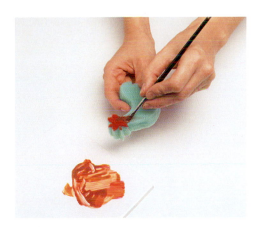

2 Trace the cockerel motif, cut it out and use it as a template to draw around on a synthetic sponge. If the sponge has a hard scourer on one side, draw on this. Cut out the cockerel using a craft knife. Paint the soft side of the sponge: paint the comb and jowls red, mix red, brown and orange together for the rest of the creature. Paint the lower edge brown.

3 Stamp the cockerel firmly onto the side of the jug.

4 Before the paint dries, use a fine paintbrush to draw the feathers in the paint. Wipe off the excess paint after each brush stroke. Dot the eye with a cotton bud to lift off the paint. Mix brown and grey paint together and paint the feet.

6 Stamp a second row of squares against those already stamped, making a chequered border. Leave to dry then bake the jug to harden the paint if necessary, following the paint manufacturer's instructions.

Floating Feathers Lamp Base

It may look like a finely painted antique, but the delicate feathers on this distinguished lamp are surprisingly easy to apply with a few simple brush strokes. Collect some real feathers to give you ideas for their colours, patterns and shapes. The patina of tiny cracks that give the lamp its aged character appear when crackle varnish is applied. Burnt umber oil paint is then rubbed into the cracks to emphasize them. The various coats of varnish applied to the lamp base will also colour it slightly and tone down the paint colours to give a mellow, warm overall effect.

Materials & Equipment

PENCIL

WHITE CERAMIC LAMP BASE

CERAMIC PAINTS: WHITE,
BROWN, GREY, YELLOW

FINE AND MEDIUM PAINTBRUSHES

WHITE CERAMIC TILE,
OLD PLATE OR MIXING TRAY

POLYURETHANE VARNISH

CRACKLE VARNISH

HAIR DRYER (OPTIONAL)

ARTIST'S OIL PAINT:
BURNT UMBER

KITCHEN PAPER

1 To paint a feather, start by drawing a pencil line on the lamp base for the central shaft. Paint the strands of the feather outwards and upwards from one side of the shaft.

2 To create pale dots, lift the paint off the feather before it dries by holding a clean paintbrush upright and dabbing it onto the paint. To make darker dots, simply dot a darker shade of paint onto the feather; do not apply the paint too thickly.

4 Use a fine paintbrush to paint a few strands outwards from the shaft at the base of the feather. Leave to dry then paint the shaft with a fine brush.

3 Create stripes on a feather by lifting the wet paint off with a clean paintbrush, applying the brush strokes in the same direction as the original painting.

5 Paint feathers at random all over the lamp base then set it aside to dry. Apply one coat of polyurethane varnish for protection and as a base for the crackle varnish.

6 Follow the manufacturer's instructions to apply the crackle varnish. If you wish to speed up the drying process, use a hairdryer on its lowest setting. When the varnish is dry, rub burnt umber oil paint all over the surface and wipe off the excess with kitchen paper. The paint will remain in the cracks. Leave to dry overnight then apply a final coat of polyurethane varnish.

Aztec Fruit Platter

Stylized, geometrically shaped creatures are a popular feature of Aztec designs. These double-headed birds are typical of those to be found crafted on Aztec antiquities and traditional textiles. Ideally, choose a square piece of china to paint as its shape will echo the straight lines of the motifs. This platter was first painted in warm, earthy tones of orange and red, using a flat brush to apply strokes in all directions for a random effect. The simple border patterns and birds were then worked on top.

Materials & Equipment

FLAT AND MEDIUM
PAINTBRUSHES

CERAMIC PAINTS: ORANGE,
RED, DARK BROWN, BLACK,
WHITE AND YELLOW

WHITE CERAMIC TILE,
OLD PLATE OR MIXING TRAY

SQUARE WHITE CERAMIC
PLATTER

MASKING TAPE OR SQUARE
PIECE OF CARD

PAPER

HARD PENCIL

SCISSORS

KITCHEN PAPER

1 Use a wide, flat paintbrush to paint the platter orange, applying the brush strokes in all directions. Set aside to dry.

2 Mask off a central square with masking tape (Test first on an old piece of china or a ceramic tile that the tape will not lift off the paint underneath. If it does, hold a square of card firmly on the platter instead.) Mix orange and red paint together. Use a wide, flat paintbrush to paint the platter around the square, applying the brush strokes in all directions as before. Leave to dry then carefully peel off the tape.

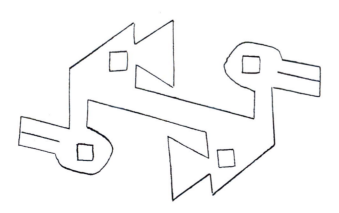

4 Cut the bird template from paper. Position the bird centrally on one side of the platter and draw around it with a hard pencil, scratching into the paint with the pencil point. Repeat on the other three sides of the platter.

3 Use a 5mm/¼in flat paintbrush to paint a zig-zag border in dark brown paint along the edges of the square.

5 Mix black with a little white paint and paint the birds. Mix white with a touch of yellow paint and paint squares on the birds. Leave to dry then paint a smaller orange square in the centre of each square.

6 Mix red and dark brown paint together. Use a 5mm/¼in flat paintbrush to paint a border of straight-sided 'S' shapes close to the outer edge, then paint a row of dashes between them. Bake the platter if necessary to harden the paint, following the paint manufacturer's instructions.

Easter Breakfast Set

This pretty breakfast china is decorated, appropriately, with delicately coloured eggs. The designs are stencilled using a brush to give a soft, stippled texture, over which dappled markings are applied using a synthetic sponge. This gives a fairly regular result, but if you would prefer more random markings, choose a sponge with large, irregular holes or use a natural sponge. Paint the rims of the egg cups and saucers in matching colours for a perfect finish. Decorated in a range of fresh spring colours, a set of this china would make a lovely Easter present.

Materials & Equipment

PAPER

PENCIL

SCISSORS

STICKY-BACKED PLASTIC

WHITE SAUCERS OR SMALL
PLATES

WHITE EGG CUPS

CERAMIC PAINTS: WHITE,
TURQUOISE, AMBER, PINK
AND DARK GREY

WHITE CERAMIC TILE,
OLD PLATE OR MIXING TRAY

STENCIL BRUSH

SYNTHETIC SPONGE

WATER OR WHITE SPIRIT

KITCHEN PAPER

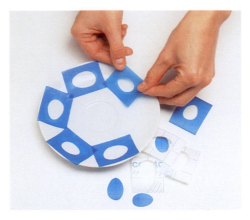

1 Make a paper template of the egg shape, scaling it to suit your china. On the paper backing of a piece of sticky-backed plastic, draw round the template to make six egg shapes for each saucer or plate, leaving a wide border around each egg. Draw one egg for each egg cup. To make the stencils, cut a rectangle around each egg, then cut out the egg. Peel off the backing paper and stick the stencils, evenly spaced, around the rim of the saucer. Stick the remaining stencil upright on the side of the egg cup.

2 Stick scraps of sticky-backed plastic around the stencils so that the surface around the egg shapes is protected from paint. Mix white paint with turquoise, amber and pink paint. Dab lightly at the first colour with a stencil brush then, holding the brush upright, apply the paint through the stencils, moving the brush in a circular motion. Stencil two eggs in each colour around the saucer.

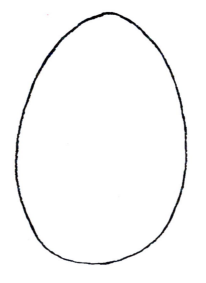

4 Tear off a piece of sponge and moisten it lightly. Use water if you are using water-based paints, or white spirit if you are using oil-based paints. Mix a little dark grey paint with each of the colours used to paint the eggs. Dab at the paint with the sponge and lightly dab the eggs to make random dappled markings. Clean the sponge, or use a fresh piece, each time you change colour.

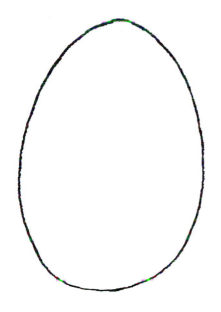

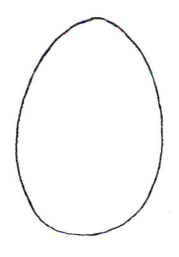

3 Stipple around the edge of each egg with turquoise, amber or pink paint, undiluted with white. This will create some realistic shading.

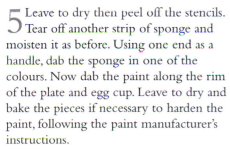

5 Leave to dry then peel off the stencils. Tear off another strip of sponge and moisten it as before. Using one end as a handle, dab the sponge in one of the colours. Now dab the paint along the rim of the plate and egg cup. Leave to dry and bake the pieces if necessary to harden the paint, following the paint manufacturer's instructions.

Dessert Plates

These pretty plates will never be completely empty, as each has its own enticing cake. This china has an embossed lattice-work rim which is ideal for painting the chequered border evenly. Decorated in fresh, sugared almond colours, the plates make a lovely dessert service or are equally appropriate for serving cakes and pastries at tea-time. Paint each plate rim in a different shade to make a charming harlequin set, or use a single, beautiful colour for the whole set. The realistic sponge texture of the cakes is actually stamped with a synthetic sponge; choose one with large, irregular holes to work the design really convincingly.

Materials & Equipment

TRACING PAPER

PENCIL

SCISSORS

FELT-TIPPED PEN

SYNTHETIC OR NATURAL
SPONGE

CRAFT KNIFE

CUTTING MAT

CERAMIC PAINTS: YELLOW,
ORANGE, WHITE, PINK,
TURQUOISE, LIGHT GREEN,
RED AND MID GREEN

WHITE CERAMIC TILE,
OLD PLATE OR MIXING TRAY

FLAT, ROUND AND FINE
PAINTBRUSHES

WHITE CERAMIC DESSERT PLATES

CHINAGRAPH PENCIL

COTTON BUD

KITCHEN PAPER

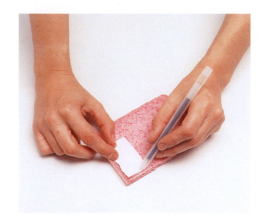

1 Trace the cakes onto tracing paper to make templates. Cut out the cakes, cutting out the separate sections. Draw around the 'sponge' parts of the cakes on a synthetic sponge. Cut out the sponge shapes to use as stamps.

2 Mix yellow with a little orange and white paint and paint onto a sponge stamp. Press the stamp firmly onto the plate. If necessary, hold a paintbrush upright to stipple more paint into any large gaps. Repeat on the other plates and leave to dry.

5 Mix red with a little orange paint and paint the strawberry on the slice of cake. Use a fine paintbrush to lift paint off the strawberry for the pips, wiping the excess paint off the brush after each stroke.

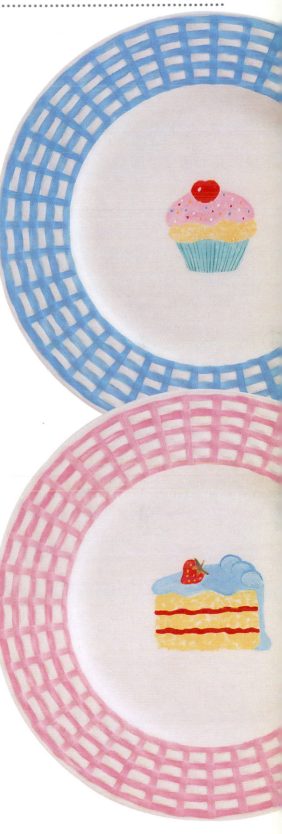

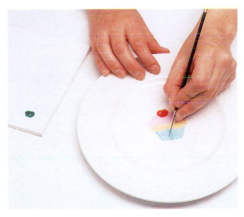

3 Place the remaining paper cake sections on the plate against the sponge and draw around them using a chinagraph pencil. To paint the icing, mix white with pink for the cupcake and white with turquoise for the slice of cake. Mix in more turquoise to paint the piped icing decorations on the slice of cake and more white to paint the highlights.

4 Paint the cherry on the cupcake red, and use a cotton bud to dab off a spot of paint to make a highlight. Mix light green and white paint together and use a flat paintbrush to paint the paper case. Leave to dry, then paint the corrugations in light green, using a fine paintbrush.

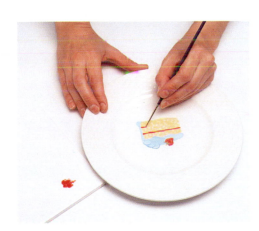

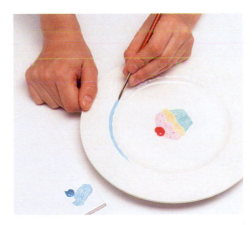

6 Paint the strawberry leaf and stalk mid green. Dot yellow paint on the pips using a fine paintbrush. Paint two rows of 'jam' on the slice of cake with red paint. Use a fine paintbrush to dot white, pink and turquoise paint on the icing of the cupcake.

7 Mix pink and white paint together for the slice of cake plate and turquoise and white paint together for the cupcake plate. Paint bands around the circumference of the plate, then paint stripes radiating outwards across the bands to make a chequered border. Leave to dry, then bake the plates if necessary to harden the paint, following the paint manufacturer's instructions.

Recycled Ceramics

Most of us have a few odd cups lacking their saucers,

or bowls that are the sole survivors of a set. They can be

put to new use as pretty containers for small plants and

cuttings. Even mugs and jugs that have broken handles

can be used for this purpose, as the damaged areas can

be turned to the back out of sight, and any chips in the

edges will be hidden by foliage and flowers. Here, floral

motifs have been used to decorate the china ready for

its new use: the bowl is rimmed with charming

erigeron flowers painted freehand and the cups

have a dramatic lily and a passion flower.

Materials & Equipment

WHITE CERAMIC BOWL AND CUPS

CERAMIC PAINTS: YELLOW,
MAUVE, FUCHSIA PINK, WHITE,
ORANGE, LIGHT BROWN,
GREEN, RED AND BLUE

MEDIUM AND FINE PAINTBRUSHES

WHITE CERAMIC TILE,
OLD PLATE OR MIXING TRAY

TRACING PAPER

PENCIL

CARBON PAPER

MASKING TAPE

KITCHEN PAPER

1 Around the bowl, paint eight circles with yellow paint, evenly spaced, for the flower centres. Mix mauve, fuchsia pink and white paint together. Paint the petals radiating outwards from the circles.

2 Hold a medium paintbrush upright to stipple orange and light brown paint onto the flower centres as stamens. Paint the stems green with a gentle, wavy line using a fine paintbrush.

4 Paint a lily petal white, rubbing away the transferred outline as you work. Before the paint dries, mix red and white together and paint along the centre of the petal towards the tip, blending the paint outwards. Leave to dry, then paint the other petals in the same way.

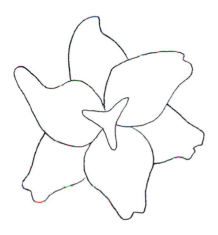

3 Trace the lily and passion flower onto tracing paper. Slip a piece of carbon paper underneath and tape it to the cups, ink side down. Redraw to transfer the design. Remove the papers. Mix green, yellow and white paint together and paint the centre of the lily, rubbing away the transferred outline with a moistened paintbrush before you colour each section.

5 With green paint, paint a curved line from the centre of the lily for the stigma stalk. Paint the stigma at the end brown. Mix red with a little blue paint and use a fine paintbrush to paint two fine lines along each petal, then dot the petals at random. Dot red paint onto the petals too.

6 Mix white with a touch of mauve paint and paint the passion flower petals, adding a little more mauve paint at the tips and on the lower layer of petals. Paint five stigmas green. Mix fuchsia pink paint with a little mauve and paint three more stigmas. Dot white paint on the flower centre. Mix black, red and mauve paint together and use a fine paintbrush to paint a halo of radiating lines around the flower centre.

7 Leave to dry, then mix mauve and fuchsia pink paint together and paint another halo of longer lines around the first. Set the china aside to dry, then bake if necessary to harden the paint, following the paint manufacturer's instructions.

Seaside Bathroom Duo

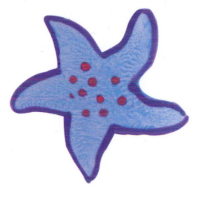

An assortment of nautical creatures decorates this

jaunty matching toothmug and soapdish. Match the

colours to your bathroom, but don't despair if you can't

find plain ceramics in the right shade. Instead of

working on coloured china, you can buy a white mug

and dish and paint the background first, which will

ensure that you have the exact colour you want. The

fish and shell designs are applied with stamps cut from

foam then outlined and decorated in co-ordinating

colours. This stamping technique gives the motifs an

attractive texture as well as providing a guide for

the freehand painting of the details.

Materials & Equipment

TRACING PAPER

PENCIL

SCISSORS

NEOPRENE FOAM

SCRAP OF CORRUGATED CARD

ALL-PURPOSE HOUSEHOLD GLUE

CERAMIC PAINTS: TURQUOISE,
FUCHSIA PINK AND MAUVE

MEDIUM AND FINE PAINTBRUSHES

LILAC CERAMIC SOAP DISH
AND BEAKER

COTTON BUD

KITCHEN PAPER

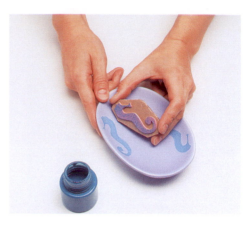

1 Trace the templates for the seahorse, large and small starfish, crab and shell and cut them out. Draw around them onto a piece of neoprene foam. Cut out the motifs and stick them to corrugated card using all-purpose household glue. Cut out the card, leaving a 5mm/¼in margin around each motif.

2 Paint the seahorse turquoise. Press the stamp firmly onto one long edge of the soap dish, close to the rim. Paint the seahorse stamp again and stamp it on the opposite long edge of the dish.

5 Leave all the motifs to dry, then outline them with mauve paint using a fine paintbrush. Paint the eye stalks on the crabs using mauve paint.

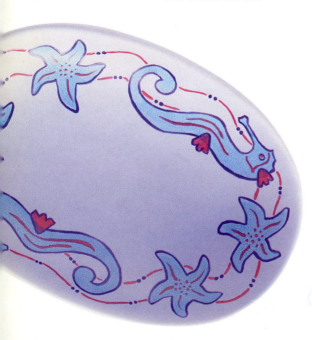

3 Before the paint dries, dot each eye with a cotton bud to lift off the paint. Using fuchsia pink paint, paint two fins on each seahorse, with three brush strokes for each fin. Paint the large starfish turquoise and stamp it a few times between the seahorses.

4 Paint the crab and shell turquoise and stamp them alternately below the rim of the beaker. Paint the small starfish turquoise and stamp it at random on the beaker.

6 Use a fine paintbrush to dot the eyes and paint details in fuchsia pink on the motifs.

7 Paint two wavy rows of dots and dashes using fuchsia pink and mauve paint. If necessary, bake the ceramics to harden the paint, following the paint manufacturer's instructions.

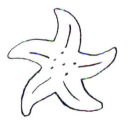

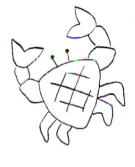

Juggling Clown Mugs

Paint some jolly clowns marching around your mugs to brighten up morning coffee breaks. Although the painting style is free and easy, looking as if it needs a very confident brush, the clown shape is actually achieved using a template. The background colour is applied using a reverse stencilling technique – the clown is cut from sticky-backed plastic and applied to the mug first. Once the background is complete, the plastic is peeled off to reveal a perfect outline ready for painting. Using semi-opaque paints means the brush strokes remain visible and form part of the design. The juggling balls are easily stamped, using the eraser on the end of a pencil.

Materials & Equipment

TRACING PAPER

HARD AND SOFT PENCILS

STICKY-BACKED PLASTIC

SCISSORS

WHITE CERAMIC MUGS

KITCHEN PAPER

SUPPORT FOR MUG HANDLES,
SUCH AS A REEL OF TAPE

FLAT AND FINE PAINTBRUSHES

SEMI-OPAQUE CERAMIC PAINTS:
YELLOW, ORANGE, RED,
TURQUOISE, PINK AND BLACK

WHITE CERAMIC TILE, OLD PLATE
OR MIXING TRAY

ERASER-ENDED PENCIL

1 Trace the clown template. Rub over the back of the tracing with a soft pencil and transfer the design to the paper backing of a piece of sticky-backed plastic. Cut out the clown. Peel off the backing paper and stick the image to the front of a mug, leaving enough space above the clown for the juggling balls. If you are making a pair of mugs, you may prefer to cut a reverse image of the clown for the other mug.

2 Place the mug face upwards on a few sheets of kitchen paper. To keep the image level, rest the handle on a suitable support such as a tape reel. Use a wide paintbrush to paint the mug in vertical brush strokes using yellow or orange paint. Leave to dry then turn the mug to continue painting the other side.

6 Use a fine paintbrush to paint corkscrew curls, then add the facial features, using red for the nose and smile and black for the eyes.

3 When the background is dry, peel off the plastic to reveal the unpainted clown shape beneath. Refer to the template to paint the frill and hat.

4 Paint the clown's outfit and boots with bold brush strokes. Don't worry about these showing, but use them to give structure to the body shape.

5 Dab the eraser on the end of a pencil into some paint. Referring to the template, stamp the eraser on to the mug above the clown to paint the juggling balls.

7 Leave the paint to dry then paint the handle using the wide paintbrush. Bake the mug if necessary to harden the paint, following the paint manufacturer's instructions.

Orange Tree Tray

Various techniques are used to decorate this tiled tray, although painting skills are not necessary as the leaves and oranges are applied with stamps made from potatoes and carrots. The design is edged with a malachite stone effect which is easy and fun to paint.

The tiles are arranged together to form a picture, which could equally well be used as a splashback or as the centrepiece of a tiled tabletop. They should be cemented in place and grouted after the picture is complete. This wooden tray was first painted white then given a wash of thinned brown paint to co-ordinate with the tree trunk and branches.

Materials & Equipment

TWELVE 10CM/4IN WHITE
CERAMIC TILES

1CM/½IN MASKING TAPE

CERAMIC PAINTS: BLACK,
WHITE, ORANGE, RED, BRIGHT
GREEN, SAGE GREEN, BROWN,
BLUE AND TURQUOISE

WHITE CERAMIC TILE, OLD PLATE
OR MIXING TRAY

FLAT, MEDIUM AND FAN
PAINTBRUSHES

KNIFE

CARROT

PAPER

SOFT PENCIL

POTATO

WATERPROOF MARKER PEN

KITCHEN PAPER

1 Arrange the tiles edge to edge in a rectangle three tiles wide and four deep. Stick 1cm/½in masking tape 2.5cm/1in within the outer edges to create a border.

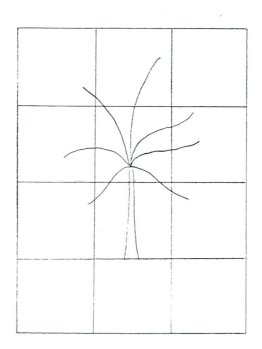

2 Mix black and white paint together to make grey. Use a 5mm/¼in wide flat paintbrush to paint the struts on the planter. Cut a slice of carrot near the tip and paint the cut surface. Leave to dry then paint again and stamp onto the tile at the top of the planter to print a pair of finials. Paint brown lines between the struts.

4 Next, hold the knife horizontally to cut around each leaf, approximately 5mm/¼in below the surface. Pull off the cut pieces of potato, leaving the leaf standing proud. Trim the sides of the potato to leave a border about 5mm/¼in wide around each stamp.

3 Trace the large leaf and cut out to make a template. Cut two thick slices from a potato. Using a waterproof marker pen, draw around the leaf on the cut faces, flipping the template to make a symmetrical pair. Hold the knife upright and cut along the outlines.

5 With a soft pencil, draw the trunk and branches of the tree freehand on the tiles, referring to the diagram. Cut a slice of carrot about 2cm/³⁄₄in in diameter for the oranges. Mix orange with a little red paint and paint the cut surface of the carrot. Paint the potato stamp bright green. Leave to dry then paint again. Press the oranges onto the tiles, followed by the leaves, rubbing away the pencil marks as you work and repainting the stamps between applications. Work the leaves outwards along the branches.

6 Paint the trunk and branches brown. Trace the small leaf onto paper and use it as a template to make a potato stamp as before. Paint the stamp sage green, leave to dry then paint again. Stamp the leaves five to six times on each side of the planter. Leave to dry. Paint along the centre of the large leaves in bright green then paint the small leaf stems sage green.

7 Paint the background within the taped border orange, using a flat paintbrush to apply the paint in all directions. To paint the outer border, hold the fan paintbrush almost horizontal so that the bristles splay open on the tiles and turn the brush in a semicircle to distribute blue and turquoise paint in fan shapes. Overlap the fans and work some of them in irregular shapes. Leave to dry, then peel off the masking tape and bake the tiles if necessary to harden the paint, following the paint manufacturer's instructions.

Hallowe'en Tureen

Sunflowers and pumpkins both appear in the garden in the golden days of autumn, so are ideal companions on this glorious tureen. The colours and silhouettes of these motifs are immediately recognizable against the rich blue background, so if you feel that adding shading to the pumpkins may be too advanced a technique for you, just paint them orange – they will still look very effective. Do not be nervous about painting a large piece of china. Although this project will take time to complete, it can be painted in easy stages and the result will be worth waiting for.

Materials & Equipment

PAPER

PENCIL

SCISSORS

MASKING TAPE

WHITE CERAMIC TUREEN

CHINAGRAPH PENCIL

KITCHEN PAPER

CERAMIC PAINTS: YELLOW,
ORANGE, LIGHT BROWN, DARK
BROWN, RED, WHITE, MID GREEN,
BRIGHT GREEN AND BLUE

FLAT, MEDIUM AND FINE
PAINTBRUSHES

WHITE CERAMIC TILE,
OLD PLATE OR MIXING TRAY

1 Trace the templates and cut out five circles for sunflowers, and three large and three small pumpkins. Cut out the centres of the sunflowers. Tape the sunflowers around the lid and the pumpkins around the tureen, alternating the sizes of the pumpkins. Draw around each template using a chinagraph pencil, then remove the templates.

2 Use kitchen paper to rub away the pencil marks on a section of a sunflower. Paint the petals outwards from the inner circle with yellow paint. Before the paint dries, add a little orange paint to each petal, close to the base. Paint the rest of the petals, rubbing away the pencil marks as you go.

4 Refer to the templates to paint the pumpkins. Either paint the sections freehand or lightly draw them first using a chinagraph pencil. Paint each section orange, blending in a band of yellow near the top as a highlight and red at the base of the pumpkin as shadow.

3 Paint the flower centres light brown. Hold a medium paintbrush upright to stipple dark brown paint in a circle in the middle, then stipple a ring around the circle.

5 Mix light brown and white paint together to paint the stalks. Mix red with a little orange and use a fine paintbrush to paint lines between the pumpkin sections to give them definition.

6 Paint a row of leaves on the rim of the lid and on the knob or handle with mid green paint. Paint the veins bright green using a fine paintbrush.

7 Rub away any visible pencil marks on the tureen and lid. Use a flat paintbrush to paint the background blue. Leave to dry then bake if necessary to harden the paint, following the paint manufacturer's instructions.

Vegetable Plot Pot Stand

This plain white tile has been transformed into a sweet little vegetable plot – there is even a rabbit stealing carrots! Designed as a pot stand, it would make a lovely gift for a keen gardener, especially if you adapted the design to resemble the recipient's own vegetable garden. The design was transferred to the tile using a pencil, as in this case the ceramic surface was not particularly shiny. You will need to experiment before transferring your design in this way, as pencil will not adhere well to very highly glazed ceramics. If this proves to be a problem, use the carbon paper transfer method described on page 16.

Materials & Equipment

SCISSORS

TRACING PAPER

SOFT AND HARD PENCILS

15CM/6IN WHITE CERAMIC TILE

CERAMIC PAINTS: YELLOW,
BROWN, WHITE, GREY, LIGHT
GREEN, MID GREEN, RED,
BLUE AND ORANGE

MEDIUM AND FINE PAINTBRUSHES

WHITE CERAMIC TILE,
OLD PLATE OR MIXING TRAY

KITCHEN PAPER

1 Cut a 15cm/6in square of tracing paper. Trace the design onto the tracing paper with a soft, sharp pencil. Lay the tracing, pencil side down, on the tile, and redraw the design with a hard pencil to transfer the image.

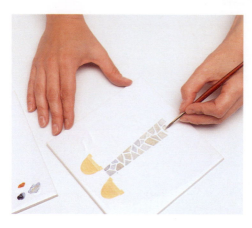

2 Mix yellow with a little brown and white paint and paint the beehives. Mix grey with a little white paint and paint some crazy paving stones between the broken lines. Add a touch of brown paint for some of the paving stones.

4 Use a fine paintbrush to paint the grasses green and the stem and branches of the bushes brown. Dip a paintbrush sparingly in green paint and dab onto the bushes to suggest leaves.

3 Now paint the vegetables, the shells and the rabbit. Mix red with a touch of blue paint to make a suitable shade for the beetroot. To paint the marrows, mix white with a little yellow paint to make a cream colour. Paint the marrows then hold a medium paintbrush upright to stipple stripes of green paint.

5 Hold a paintbrush upright to stipple light green paint on the hedge within the broken lines. Stipple mid green paint on top in some areas for shading.

6 Paint the details with a fine paintbrush: add shades of green foliage to the beetroots and carrots and yellow dots to the grasses to suggest flowers. Leave to dry then bake the tile if necessary to harden the paint, following the paint manufacturer's instructions.

Oriental Tableware

Authentic Chinese ceramics are inexpensive to buy

and their simple, curvaceous lines are always appealing.

They lend themselves to lots of painting possibilities.

This smart group of ceramics has a distinctive fishing

theme, influenced by free-flowing Chinese brushwork.

There is a flamboyant fish, a lively prawn and a

fisherman wending his way homeward with a mighty

catch. Even the spoon has a delicate representation

of a boatman fishing from his boat. The vibrant shades

of red used throughout link all the pieces to

form a matching set.

Materials & Equipment

PAIR OF COMPASSES

STICKY-BACKED PLASTIC

SCISSORS

WHITE CERAMIC CUP, DISH,
BOWL AND SPOON

SYNTHETIC SPONGE

CERAMIC PAINTS: RED, BLACK,
WHITE, BLUE AND ORANGE

MEDIUM AND FINE PAINTBRUSHES

TRACING PAPER

PENCIL

CARBON PAPER

MASKING TAPE

WHITE CERAMIC TILE,
OLD PLATE OR MIXING TRAY

CHINAGRAPH PENCIL

KITCHEN PAPER

1 Draw a 4cm/1½in diameter circle on the paper backing of a sheet of sticky-backed plastic and cut it out. Peel off the paper backing then stick the circle to the cup. Paint a synthetic sponge red and dab it all over the cup to build up an even covering of paint. Allow to dry then peel off the circle.

2 Trace the fisherman template onto tracing paper. Cut a 4cm/1½in diameter circle of carbon paper and place it, ink side down, over the circle on the cup. Tape the tracing on top. Redraw the image to transfer it to the cup. Remove the papers. Mix black with a little white paint to paint the fisherman dark grey using a fine paintbrush.

5 Sponge the inside and the base of the bowl red and leave to dry. Trace the prawn template and cut it out. Draw around the prawn on the front of the bowl with a chinagraph pencil. Paint each section of the prawn red. Before the paint dries on the head, mix a little black paint with the red and paint a short stripe from the front of the head towards the body, then paint a tail fin at the end of the body. Paint a red tail fin at each side.

3 Trace the fish template. Place the tracing on top of a sheet of carbon paper and cut out the circle through both layers. To allow the template to sit smoothly inside the dish, hold the circles together and make a series of cuts from the circumference in towards the centre.

4 Place the template and carbon in the dish, ink side down. The cuts will overlap to fit the shape of the dish. Tape in position. Redraw the fish to transfer it to the china, then remove the papers. Paint the fish red, wiping away the transferred outlines with a moistened paintbrush before painting each line. Mix a touch of blue into the red paint to paint, freehand, the tail fins, the centre of the eye, the rim of the dish and some reeds. Mix red and orange paint together to paint the details on the fish and reeds.

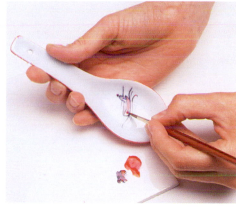

6 Paint the legs and claws red. Paint the eyes and feelers black. Mix red with a little black paint and use a fine paintbrush to apply short feathery brush strokes outwards from the body.

7 Sponge the underside of the spoon red. Trace the boatman onto tracing paper. Place a piece of carbon paper in the spoon, ink side down, and tape the tracing on top. Redraw to transfer the design. Remove the papers. Paint the design black with a fine paintbrush. Paint the interior of the boat red mixed with a touch of black. Paint the exterior of the boat red. Leave to dry, then bake the china if necessary to harden the paint, following the paint manufacturer's instructions.

Moorish Coffee Pot

The vibrant colours used on this chic coffee pot give a contemporary twist to its Moorish theme. A variety of techniques have been used and if you are in the mood for some complex painting, this is definitely a project to go for. The regal camel, laden with a smart tasselled carpet, is framed within a Moroccan arch, and the pot is bordered with a simple motif often found on oriental carpets. This border would also work well alone on a plain piece of china, perhaps worked in subdued colours if you would prefer a simpler, classic style.

Materials & Equipment

2.5CM/1IN AND 2CM/¾IN
MASKING TAPE

WHITE CERAMIC COFFEE POT

SCISSORS

TRACING PAPER

SOFT AND HARD PENCILS

STICKY-BACKED PLASTIC

CRAFT KNIFE

CUTTING MAT

SUPPORT, SUCH AS
A TAPE REEL

FLAT, MEDIUM AND FINE
PAINTBRUSHES

CERAMIC PAINTS: FUCHSIA PINK,
BLUE, WHITE, LIGHT BROWN,
YELLOW, GREEN, TURQUOISE,
RED, MAUVE, DARK BROWN
AND GOLD

CARBON PAPER

WHITE CERAMIC TILE, OLD PLATE
OR MIXING TRAY

KITCHEN PAPER

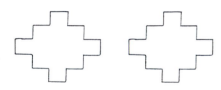

1 Stick 2.5cm/1in masking tape around the top of the pot and the end of the spout. Then stick 2cm/¾in masking tape along the handle and around the knob on the lid. Press the tape down well, smoothing out any creases that form on the curves of the china.

2 Trace the arch template onto tracing paper using a soft pencil. Tape the tracing, face down, on the paper backing of a sheet of sticky-backed plastic and redraw it to transfer the design. Remove the tracing. Cut out the arch with a craft knife on a cutting mat. Peel off the paper backing and stick the arch centrally to one side of the coffee pot.

5 Remove the tracing and carbon paper. Mix blue and white paint together. Use a 5mm/¼in wide flat paintbrush to paint a frame within the arch. Paint the camel design. Using gold paint, add dots to the sky as stars, a fringe to the blanket and a disc to the harness. Use a fine paintbrush to paint the camel's facial features dark brown, then paint gold stars at random on the pot and lid.

3 Remove the lid and stand the pot on a support such as a tape reel to lift it off the work surface. Use a flat paintbrush to paint the pot and lid all over with fuchsia pink paint, applying the brush strokes in all directions. Leave to dry and apply a second coat in the same way for a stronger colour. Peel off the arch stencil.

4 Trace the camel motif onto tracing paper and cut out along the broken lines. Cut the arch from carbon paper, cutting along the broken lines. Position the carbon paper, ink side down, centrally within the arch on the pot. Then tape the camel tracing on top and redraw to transfer the design.

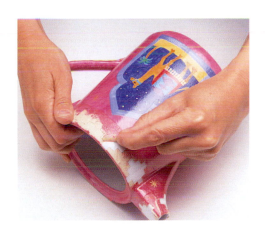

6 Trace the border motif onto tracing paper and cut it out. Draw around the motif eight times on the wide masking tape border around the pot and twice on the tape on the spout, spacing the motifs evenly. Cut along the outlines with a craft knife. Peel off the motifs.

7 Use a flat paintbrush to paint the motifs turquoise, applying the paint in the direction of the tape so it does not spread over the pink paint. Now draw a row of diamonds on the tape on the handle and lid knob. Cut along the outlines with a craft knife and peel off the diamonds. Paint them red and leave to dry.

8 Remove the remaining pieces of masking tape. Paint the revealed areas mauve on the wide borders and mauve and blue on the narrow borders. There is no need to paint right up to the motifs. Leave to dry then, with a fine paintbrush, paint a gold line around each motif and a gold dot in the centre. Bake the pot if necessary to harden the paint, following the paint manufacturer's instructions.

Indian
Coasters

Mehndi is an ancient and important part of a South

Indian marriage ceremony, where leaves from the

henna plant are made into a dye and used to paint

beautifully intricate designs on the hands and feet of

the bride. These coasters are inspired by the wonderful

Mehndi designs. Here, the images are applied to yellow

ceramic tiles using outliner, in colours that echo the

warmth of henna while enhancing the design with a

subtle metallic sheen. Follow the colourwashing

technique described on page 17 if you would prefer

to use white tiles and colour them yourself.

Materials & Equipment

TRACING PAPER

PENCIL

SCISSORS

CARBON PAPER

10CM/4IN YELLOW CERAMIC TILES

MASKING TAPE

CERAMIC OUTLINER: COPPER
OR VERMEIL

STICKY-BACKED FELT

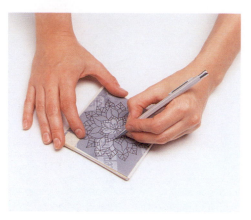

1 Trace the design onto tracing paper. Cut a square of carbon paper slightly smaller than the tile. Position the carbon paper ink side down on the tile then tape the tracing on top.

2 Redraw the design with a pencil to transfer the image. Remove the tracing and carbon paper.

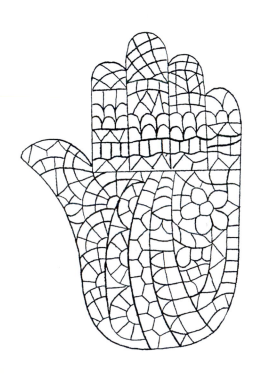

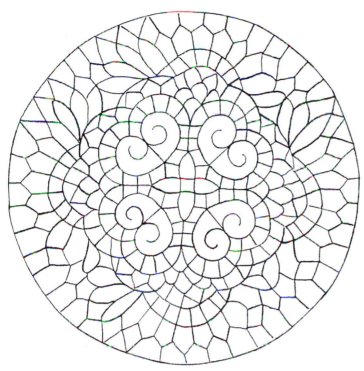

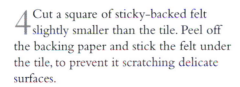

3 Trace along the design with the outliner, taking care to apply an even pressure on the tube. Set aside for 24 hours to harden, then bake the coasters following the paint manufacturer's instructions.

4 Cut a square of sticky-backed felt slightly smaller than the tile. Peel off the backing paper and stick the felt under the tile, to prevent it scratching delicate surfaces.

Beachcomber's Boxes

These elegant ceramic boxes have been turned into

practical storage jars with the addition of smart metal

lids. Aluminium foil, which is available from craft

suppliers, is shaped by embossing the fold lines with an

empty ballpoint pen. Cut the foil with an old pair of

scissors as the metal will blunt the blades. Ceramic

beads make an ideal finishing touch as knobs to lift the

lids – and remember that you can paint the beads to

match the box if you cannot find the right colour.

Pebbles and shells are painted onto the containers

as a reminder of idyllic beach holidays.

Materials & Equipment

WHITE CERAMIC SQUARE OR
RECTANGULAR BOXES

CHINAGRAPH PENCIL

3 FINE ELASTIC BANDS

CERAMIC PAINTS: BLACK, WHITE,
LIGHT BROWN, DARK BROWN,
RED AND ORANGE

MEDIUM AND FINE PAINTBRUSHES

WHITE CERAMIC TILE,
OLD PLATE OR MIXING TRAY

KITCHEN PAPER

TRACING PAPER

PENCIL

MASKING TAPE

CARBON PAPER

ALUMINIUM FOIL

BALLPOINT PEN

OLD PAIR OF SCISSORS

ALL-PURPOSE HOUSEHOLD GLUE

BRASS PAPER FASTENERS

CERAMIC BEADS WITH
LARGE HOLES

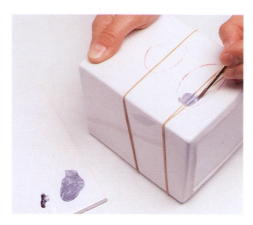

1 Draw two oval pebble shapes on the front of a box using a chinagraph pencil. Slip three narrow elastic bands over the box and arrange them on the pebbles as 'fault lines'. Mix black and white paint together and paint the pebbles. Leave to dry then mix in a little more black to stipple the edges as shadow. Add more white and stipple a highlight across the centre. Leave to dry then remove the elastic bands.

2 Trace the shells onto tracing paper. Stick the tracings to the boxes with masking tape and slip a piece of carbon paper underneath each one, ink side down. Redraw to transfer the designs (do not transfer the streaks on the nautilus shell). Remove the papers. Mix white with a touch of light brown paint and paint the patterns on the cone shell. Paint the background dark brown and blend the browns and white together to paint the other areas.

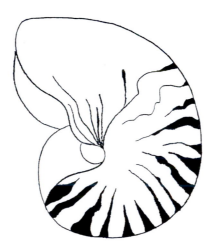

6 Fold the hems along the embossed lines then fold along the remaining lines, tucking the tabs inside. Glue the tabs under the sides of the lid.

3 Paint the nautilus shell. If you do not feel confident about blending the colours together on the shell, simply paint the areas in blocks of solid colour. Mix red, orange and light brown paint together then refer to the template to paint the streaks using a fine paintbrush. Leave to dry, then bake the boxes if necessary to harden the paint, following the paint manufacturer's instructions.

4 To make a lid, rest the upturned box on a few sheets of kitchen paper and the aluminium foil. Draw around it firmly on the metal using a ballpoint pen. Remove the box.

5 Referring to the diagram, draw a 2.5cm/1in border around the box outline, then draw the tab lines and 8mm/$\frac{3}{8}$in hems. Snip to the box outline along the thicker lines. Pierce a hole in the centre of the lid with the points of the scissors.

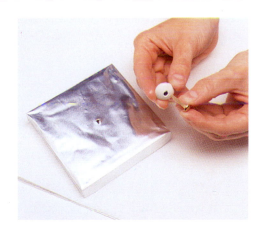

7 Insert the prongs of a brass paper fastener through a bead. Slip the prongs through the lid hole and splay them open on the underside. Put the lid on the box.

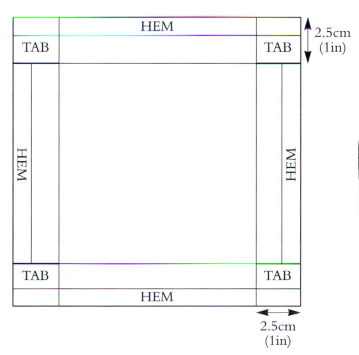

Japanese Dish

A traditional Japanese textile inspired this elegant design of a stylized bird in flight. The crane is an important motif in Japanese decorative art. Because it was once believed to live for a thousand years, this graceful bird represents long life or immortality, and has developed into a symbol of general good fortune and happiness. For this dish, the crane is stencilled and the star background is painted freehand in broad, fluid bands, giving the impression of a cloudy sky. Work the design on a plain piece of oriental-style china using dark blue ceramic paint to give it an authentic Japanese look.

Materials & Equipment

TRACING PAPER

SOFT AND HARD PENCILS

MASKING TAPE

STICKY-BACKED PLASTIC

CRAFT KNIFE

CUTTING MAT

PALE GREY SQUARE
CERAMIC DISH

CERAMIC PAINT: DARK BLUE

WHITE CERAMIC TILE,
OLD PLATE OR MIXING TRAY

FLAT AND FINE PAINTBRUSHES

STENCIL BRUSH

CHINAGRAPH PENCIL

KITCHEN PAPER

1 Trace the template onto tracing paper using a soft pencil. Tape the tracing, face down, on the paper backing of a piece of sticky-backed plastic and redraw it to transfer the design. Remove the tracing. Cut out the shapes with a craft knife resting on a cutting mat.

2 Peel back one corner of the paper backing and position the stencil centrally on the dish, sticking the corner in place. Peel back the rest of the paper as you stick the stencil to the dish, smoothing the plastic outwards to expel any air bubbles.

3 Apply a thin film of dark blue paint to a tile or an old plate using a flat paintbrush. Dab lightly at the paint with a stencil brush. Then hold the brush upright to apply paint through the stencil, moving the brush with a circular motion. Set aside to dry, then carefully peel off the stencil.

4 Draw irregular undulating shapes on the dish around the bird using a chinagraph pencil, to mark the areas to be painted with the background design. Refer to the photograph on page 126 to see how to position the shapes.

5 Use a fine paintbrush to paint a repeat design of starbursts within the marked areas, trying to keep them regular in size. Rub away the pencil lines when the paint has dried. Bake the dish if necessary to harden the paint, following the paint manufacturer's instructions.

Index

ACKNOWLEDGEMENTS

Special thanks to Fiona Eaton and Alison Myer at David & Charles for their enthusiasm and support. Also thanks to Amanda Heywood for the beautifully styled photographs and to her assistants, Vanessa and Karen, for all their help.

RESOURCES

DMC Creative World Ltd
Pullman Road
Wigston
Leicestershire LE18 2DY
Tel: 0116 281 1040
(ceramic painting kits; contact for your nearest stockist)

Forbo CP Ltd.
Station Road
Cramlington
Northumberland NE23 8AQ
Tel: 01670 718222
(Fablon sticky-backed plastic; contact for your nearest stockist)

Homecrafts Direct
PO Box 38
Leicester LE1 9BU
Tel: 0116 251 3139
(ceramic paints; mail order available)

Philip and Tacey Ltd
North Way
Andover
Hampshire SP10 5BA
Tel: 01264 332171
(Pebeo water-based porcelain 150 paint and outliner; contact for your nearest stockist)